Sir M. Visvesvaraya

An Incredible Engineer

DR. R.P.RAJ

INDIA · SINGAPORE · MALAYSIA

Notion Press

No.8, 3rd Cross Street
CIT Colony, Mylapore
Chennai, Tamil Nadu – 600004

First Published by Notion Press 2020
Copyright © Dr. R.P.Raj 2020
All Rights Reserved.

ISBN 978-1-64951-949-8

This book has been published with all efforts taken to make the material error-free after the consent of the author. However, the author and the publisher do not assume and hereby disclaim any liability to any party for any loss, damage, or disruption caused by errors or omissions, whether such errors or omissions result from negligence, accident, or any other cause.

While every effort has been made to avoid any mistake or omission, this publication is being sold on the condition and understanding that neither the author nor the publishers or printers would be liable in any manner to any person by reason of any mistake or omission in this publication or for any action taken or omitted to be taken or advice rendered or accepted on the basis of this work. For any defect in printing or binding the publishers will be liable only to replace the defective copy by another copy of this work then available.

CONTENTS

Engineering Facts   5
Foreword   7
Preface   9
Acknowledgements   11

1. Early Life   15
2. The Story of Bhagiratha   17
3. College Education   19
4. Marriage   21
5. Early Job at Nashik   23
6. Sukkur Challenge   25
7. Automatic Gates – A New Invention   26
8. Block Irrigation System – as a Solution   28
9. Aden Calling   30
10. After Aden   32
11. First Retirement   33
12. Special Consultant Engineer in Hyderabad   34
13. Brief History of Hyderabad   37
14. Chief Engineer of Mysore   39
15. The King, the Dam and the Gardens   40
16. Diwan of Mysore   45

Contents

17.	University of Mysore	47
18.	State Bank of Mysore	48
19.	Bhadravathi Iron and Steel Works	49
20.	Participation in Political and Other Conferences	52
21.	Foreign Tours	54
22.	Sir MV – a Man of Simplicity	57
23.	Awards and Honours	59
24.	Sir M Visvesvaraya & Gandhi	61
25.	Sir M V and Jawaharlal Nehru	63
26.	Humorous Centurion	65
27.	Death and Legacy	66
28.	Muddena Halli Memorial	67
29.	Tales of Visvesvaraya	70
30.	Books of Sir MV	73
31.	Famous Quotes of Sir M Visvesvaraya	74
32.	Lesser Known Facts About Sir M. Visvesvaraya	76
33.	Engineers Day	78
34.	Chronology	80
35.	Sources	82
	Sir M. Visvesvaraya an Incredible Engineer	83
	About the Author	84

ENGINEERING FACTS

- 4 Years
- 40 Subjects
- 400 Experiments
- 4000 Assignments
- 40000 Hours
- A Normal Human Being Cannot Do It
- These Super Heroes Are Called Engineers.

FOREWORD

I sincerely admire the efforts of Dr. R P Raj in compiling achievements of Sir M Vishvesvaraya in a chronological order. It will be useful not only to students but to all ages as the book is handy and readable within a short time.

I hope this book is a must read for engineering students and engineers to know the contribution of Sir M Vishvesvaraya to the society. The young generation are the wealth of the nation and they should know about our National Architect Sir M Vishvesvaraya.

My heartiest congratulations on his solo herculean efforts in spite of his busy schedule as an orthopaedic surgeon.

With Best Wishes.

General Manager & Head/HPEP
BHEL, R C Puram
Hyderabad

PREFACE

While releasing my first book "THE UNDERRATED LEADER" the love shown to me by all employees of BHEL I was over whelmed with joy and found no words to express my gratitude.

On the day of the release of the book 'THE UNDERRATED LEADER' there was also a Maa TV artists function where most famous TV artists participated. Some of my own people asked me to postpone the program of my book release function and told me there would not be much attendance. But my decision was irrevocable. And to my surprise the auditorium was full of people from all walks of life who participated from the beginning till the end of the function. One of the attendees who attended the function suggested me to write a book on Sri M.Visvesvaraya. He said that the younger generation of India is spending most of their time on mobiles and TV sets focusing on film personalities. It is our duty to spread more awareness among the younger generation about the real heroes who spent their entire life for the common good of the society.

Like the saying "a little encouragement can spark a great endeavor." This has not only prompted me but also motivated me to keep the present generation aware of our National hero Sir M.Visvesvaraya. And the result is this ....'Humble book.'

Sir M.Visvesvaraya's biography is really inspiring for all the people young and old. He was not only an excellent engineer but a great human being. Each one can learn one thing or the other from his life.

        HAPPY READING

Dr. R.P.Raj

ACKNOWLEDGEMENTS

I am Thank full to

- General Manager & Head HPEP BHEL R.C Puram Shri Amit Kerketta for writing a forword for this book.
- Dr.P.P Sharma CMS and Head of Surgery BHEL General Hospital for constant Encouragement.
- To all General Managers of BHEL (HPEP)
- A Rabindranath Babu Retired GM BHEL for his whole hearted Support.
- Mrs.Sabitha for her help in writing the book.
- Kranthi for his legal advices.
- To all Doctors, Para Medical Staff for their support
- Kannada Geleyara Balaga For their constant motivation.
- Office bearers of all Trade Unions HPEP BHEL R.C Puram for their kind cooperation.
- Above all I am extremely thankful to my wife Dr.Geethanjali N, for her support and understanding.

"To give real service you must add something which cannot be bought or measured with money."

Sir.M.Visvesvaraya

EARLY LIFE

Visvesvaraya was born on 15th September, 1861 at Muddenahalli, into a Telugu speaking family in a small village near Bangalore. His father Mokshagundam Srinivas Sastry was a Sanskrit Scholar and mother Venkata lakshmamma was a pious and dutiful woman who followed all traditional practices with utmost care. His parents were from Mokshagundam, a village in Prakasham district(Andhra Pradesh).

His primary education was done at Muddenahalli Village in Chikkaballapur District Which is around 40KM away from Bangalore. When as a very young boy he was fond of staying at home and spending time with his mother rather than going to school. He absented himself from the village school for more than a month. When his uncle H. Ramaiah came to know of this matter and he severely reprimanded both Visvesvaraya and his mother. He said that if he does not go to school he will end up as a shepherd boy. And he said that God also will not help shepherds because they are the most lazy people without any goals and roaming with animals from place to place. Visvesvaraya cried after listening to his uncle's words and decided not to absent himself from school thereafter. He told his uncle that he will not become a shepherd. After that incident, he became a very punctual student and became one of the favorite students for his teachers.

His high school education completed at Mission High School at Bangalore.

From the beginning he was recognized as a bright student not only by the teachers but also by the people living around his locality. They say that his village had only one street lamp and Visvesvaraya used to study under the street lamp for many hours in the night. Once his father told young Visvesvaraya the story of Bhagiratha.

THE STORY OF BHAGIRATHA

Bhagiratha is one of the King Ikshavaku dynasty who brought the river Ganga from heaven to earth. Rama also belonged to Ikshavaku dynasty. When Bhagiratha became the prince of Sagara dynasty he came to know about his sixty thousand uncles who did not get moksha because of the curse of a holy saint. After a hard penance Lord Brahma appeared and gave him a solution for the salvation of his uncles. Lord Brahma advised Bhagiratha to meditate and please Lord Shiva so that he could help him to bring Ganga on earth. He also told Bhagiratha that when river Ganga flows over the areas where his uncles were cremated they would get moksha and go to heaven.

So Bhagiratha did hard penance to please Lord Shiva and he became successful after continuous meditation for two to three years. Shiva appeared and and offered a boon to Bhagiratha. Bhagiratha was very happy and asked Shiva to bring Ganga down to earth. Shiva agreed and let Ganga go down to earth. But Ganga was feeling proud and did not like to go to earth alone. She wanted to take Shiva along with her.

Ganga came down very robustly with a great speed with the idea of causing massive destruction to life on earth. But Shiva the protector tied down Ganga by tying the knot in his hair. Ganga was stuck down between the hair of Lord Shiva.

Again Bhagiratha did a hard penance and pleased Lord Shiva . He let go of Ganga gently on earth. The river Ganga flew gently in all directions and it is said that the river disturbed the penance of a saint Jugnu. He tied her down again to one place.

King Bhagiratha convinced Jugnu and told him his story and purpose of his life . Now Bhagiratha took Ganga along with him to where ever his sixty thousand uncles were cremated. After Ganga river flowed over them all his uncles attained salvation and reached heaven. This story of Bhagiratha told by his father where he persistently tries to bring Ganga down to earth impressed young Visvesvaraya . He also tried to build dams across the country and and tamed the water flow and stored them for irrigation and drinking purpose.

COLLEGE EDUCATION

Visvesvaraya's father Srinivas Shastri died all of a sudden leaving young Visvesvaraya in tears. His father always believed that education was important to progress in once life. He stressed upon young Visvesvaraya to studied as much as possible.After his father's death he was under the careful graduationship of his uncle H.Ramaiah his mother's brother

Visvesvaraya was only fifteen years old when his father expired. Then his uncle Ramaiah got him admitted in Mission High school (Bangalore). In 1875 Visvesvaraya completed his high school with flying colors. He joined the central college Bangalore for his higher education. During his college days itself he started tuitions to many children. He was very disciplined and punctual from his earlier days itself. . He was a sought after teacher even for children of the Ministers of Mysore Government. He used to take tuitions in the morning and walk to his uncles house for breakfast and thereafter he used to attend college which was another 4-5 miles away from his uncle's house. He used to walk a minimum of atleast 10 miles a day which became a life long ritual. When asked later in his life what is the secret of his good health he used to say that from earlier days he walked his entire life for good health.

Visvesvaraya was the most favourable student of Charles Water's an Englishman who was the then Principal of Central college. The teacher gave two gifts to his student , a Webster's dictionary and a favourite gold cuff links which he preserved them in his entire life. Visvesvaraya passed his B.A examination with distinctionand obtained a scholarship from Govt. of Mysore to pursue studies outside his state.

Visvesvaraya joined the college of science in Poona to study Engineering. He took two exams LCE and FCEL in 1883 and won the prestigious James Berkley Gold medal for getting first rank. Every rank holder of the state were offered a Government Job and similarly Visvesvaraya also got an appointment to join Public works department of Bombay and placed at Nashik district.

MARRIAGE

Marriage is a great lottery somebody rightly said. You may be lucky or unlucky within the marriage. Visvesvaraya belonged to the latter category.

When he was studying in Engineering college he was married to a girl called Saraswathi, daughter of a school teacher at Chikkaballapur. She lived with Visvesvaraya's mother most of the times as he was busy in his engineering studies. Later the couple was blessed with a baby. As the perinatal mortality was very high those days the mother and the child died because of some unknown infection.

Visvesvaraya was forced to marry again within six months after the death of his first wife. She too died during the delivery of the child.

Again his mother forced him to marry the third time even though Visvesvaraya was very reluctant. Even this marriage was a failure and they could not continue their married life. He decided not to marry again but to live alone all his life as he was not interested to marry again.

Sir M. Visvesvaraya

EARLY JOB AT NASHIK

After persuing his B.A. examinations with distinction and securing a scholarship of Govt.of Mysore to persue higher studies outside. Visvesvaraya joined the college of Science in Poona to study Engineering. He took two exams L.C.E. and F.C.E.L. in 1983 and secured first rank for the Bombay Presidency . He won the prestigious James Berkley medal for his outstanding achievement. As it was customary those days a Government job was guaranteed to rank holders. Visvesvaraya was appointed as assistant engineer in Public works department of Bombay. His first posting was at Nasik. His job included construction and repair of irrigation river channels. He was asked to build a siphon on river Panjea at Dathari village. Soon after the work he was forced to suspend the work because of heavy rains. The Government reprimanded the young engineer and told him not to give reasons for incompletion of job and that he would be labelled disobedient. Visvesvaraya accepted this challenge and eventhough his labourers were in experienced so was he. But he successfully constructed a siphon across a rocky hill. His work was highly appreciated by the same executive engineer who had earlier passed the adverse remark about him.

The Executive Engineer Mr.H.G. Pallikar encouraged Visvesvaraya to pass higher departmental exams. Visvesvaraya scored the highest and in Marathi a new language he scored the highest. He elevation to first grade engineer earned him Rs 500/- per month. His repeated ill health at Khandesh district forced for transfer. His superiors obliged him and transferred him to Poona and entrusted a new job in charge of Roads and Buildings division. He was offered a challenging work at Sukkur.

SUKKUR CHALLENGE

While Sir.M.V was working in Bombay presidency of undivided India he was asked to devise a method to supply water from river Sindh to a small town called Sukkur in 1894.Presently Sukkur is a city in Pakistan Province of Sindh along the western bank of Indus River.Sukkur is the 3rd Largest city of Pakistan after Karachi and Hyderabad.

He was already planning to provide drinking water from the river Sindh to Sukkur by pumping the river water to a nearby filters and supply to the people. Instead of constructing costly filters he got a circular well dug in a river bed and connected it to a tunnel dug under the river. Water percolating through the sands to the bottom of the well was filtered and purified and then pumped into the tank on the hill which supplied water to the public. This was a simple method, which resulted in more timely water supplies for the existing cultivated areas of Sindh province.

People of Pakistan owe him a deep depth of gratitude to Sir M. Visvesvaraya for this contribution.

AUTOMATIC GATES – A NEW INVENTION

After his service at Surat, Visvesvaraya was posted as assistant to Chief Engineer Poona Division. He was made in charge of Poona district irrigation. He was concerned with both drinking water supply to Poona and irrigation of farmlands with minimal water wastage.

A river of Musi tributary provided water to Poona and Karkee military station. It used to dry up during summers. There was no other option left except to raise the wall of a small dam but wall was not strong enough to hold excess water and it involved heavy expenses.

Visvesvaraya himself designed the automatic gates by which the storage capacity of the lake could be increased. An increase of eight feet above the original dam could hold about 25% of more water without affecting the walls. The gates could hold the excess water and whenever the water level would rise above this height the gates open automatically for the escape of the surplus water. On the other hand the water gates would close when the water level falls below the increased 8 feet. This was a wonderful creation. The Government patented this. He refused to accept any royalty to him as he was still a Government servant and would not accept any money.

Gates were also installed at the Tigra Dam in Gwalior, KRS Dam in Mysore and even some other dams. The first automatic gates were still working when Sir M. Visveswaraya visited this dam 50 years later.

BLOCK IRRIGATION SYSTEM – AS A SOLUTION

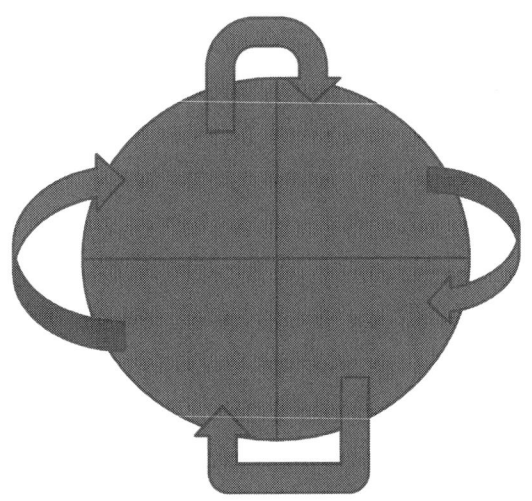

**DOWNWARD TERMINATION WAY POINT
(COURTESY Caroline paul)**

Block irrigation was used to save water in Alternative Wet and Dry irrigation [AWD]. The command area of a Deep Tube Well is much larger than a short tube well. A large Deep tube well supplies water to one or two blocks according to a Schedule.

Normally one DTW consists of 15 blocks of 15 to 17 individual plots. A DTW involves more than 100 to 200 farmers whereas a STW may supply to around 30 farmers only.

This type of irrigation can reduce the water consumption by as much as 35%. It increases the yield of the crops also. By this method we can save at least 40% of water loses due to seepage and evaporation.

Sir M Visveswaraya used this method of irrigation in many of his projects throughout the country.

ADEN CALLING

Sir M. Visvesvaraya was the first Engineer from India to be posted as Senior Engineer to any foreign country viz . Aden.

Aden is the port city and located by eastern approach to Red sea, some 170 km east of

Bob–el mandab to Aden's natural harbor lies in the crater of a dormant Volcano which now forms C peninsula joined to the mainland by a low isthmus. It was under the control of British till November 1967 and is now called Peoples Republic of south Yemen.

Aden was a military settlement port and from sea port at the entry of Suez canal from India. At that point of time Aden was under Bombay Presidency which was controlled by Britishers. Water was scarce in Aden the responsibility of providing and sanitation etc lay with the Britishers. Sir M. Visvesvaraya was asked to go to Aden to study the problem.

Sir M. Visvesvaraya went to Aden and collected information in and around Aden. He has recorded a nearby mountain about 60 miles from Aden has little rainfall. Rain water would flow down and disappear in sandy lahej 18 miles from Aden. He recommended the digging of a well there pump the water to a nearby storage tank on a hill and then supply it to Aden through pipes.

Lahej belonged to a Sultan and Visvesvaraya helped in negotiation with sultan of Lahej. Visvesvaraya also noticed that the death rates in and around Aden was very high because of frequent plagues, famines and improper drainage. He also suggested a pipe sewage system for speedy removal of sewage and was led to sea by gravitation costing very less. He also proved that death rate was comparatively low wherever underground drainage is available. Aden, Shaik Othman and Tawahi remains indebted to Sir Visvesvaraya for this marvelous idea and implementation of drainage for which he was awarded the Kaiser.I. Hind medal.

AFTER ADEN

After returning from Aden he was asked to visit the city of Kolhapur and suggest a bad leaking eastern dam and was in the danger of giving away . Mr. Visveswaraya worked day and night and repaired the dam towards absolute safety. Dewan of Kolhapur was highly impressed and conveyed this frankly to Bombay governance.

In 1907 he was placed in charge of Engineers Division in the Bombay Presidency for 6 months. While at Belgaum he prepared a set of Road Maintenance rules. Similarly water scheme Dharwad and Bijapur were prepared by him Lord Sydenham the then Governor sanctioned whatever the eminent Visvesvaraya asked because of high integrity and meritorious work too.

Visvesvaraya was given addition responsible of revising the scheme of Engineering Education at Poona where he himself had studied. The college was renamed college of Engineering.

He is credited with framing University Regulations which was accepted as soon as passed.

FIRST RETIREMENT

An Indian rising to the highest position was highly intolerable to the British officers and also his colleagues. He could see the discontentment in the office. Hence Sir Visvesvaraya announced his retirement all of a sudden. Government of Bombay wrote to Government of India on March 1908.

His Excellency the Governor in council considers that the service rendered by Mr. Visvesvaraya has been exceptionally meritorious and fully entitled him the additional pension. He was the first Indian to be granted pension and relieved gracefully with a wish for him to achieve more for his people and the country.

After his retirement he took a tour to western countries to gain more knowledge. While he was in London the Government of India sent a cable to Visvesvaraya on behalf of the Government of Hyderabad requesting his urgent services at the Nizam Government.

He told the Nizams that he would offer his services only after completion of his tour, which would take another five months and also gave them options of selecting some other person. After visiting Russia, Canada and America he returned back to India in April 1909.

SPECIAL CONSULTANT ENGINEER IN HYDERABAD

Musi River or Musinuru is one of the tributary of the river Krishna which is flowing through Telangana State. Hyderabad stands on the banks of Musi River, which divides the historic old city, and the new city of Hyderabad. Till the early 20th century Musi River was the cause of flood devastation in Hyderabad. On 28th September 1908 Hyderabad witnessed one of the disastrous floods in its history. This flood caused severe devastation in and around Hyderabad leaving lakhs of people homeless ,and also around 15,000 people were killed.

The modern era of development of twin cities Hyderabad and Secunderabad goes unabated since 1908. Abdalla Ahmed Ahmed Bin Mehfooz submitted the report of Musi floods. He requested the Nizam (Emperor) of Hyderabad to prevent the recurrence of the floods and improving the other civic amenities of the people living in Hyderabad. Nizams wrote to the British Empire and the British Empire deputed Sir. M. Visvesvaraya to look into the problem.

Sri. M. Visvesvaraya in detail studied the Musi river and came up with a blue print and discussed with Nizam. Nizam told Sri. M. Visvesvaraya that he is ready to fund the resources saying Hyderabad and its people should not face another floods like the 1908 floods. Sri. M. Visvesvaraya suggested that he would like to change the course of the Musi River itself by building two dams on its ways diverting the water flow so that the river will not enter the city directly. Nizam Vll constituted a city improvement trust in 1912. Sir M. Visvesvaraya suggested building a dam in 1920 across the river ten miles 16 km upstream from the city called Osman sagar. In 1927 another reservoir was built on ESI (tributary of Musi) and named him Himayath sagar. These lakes and dams constructed prevented the flooding of Musi River and are the major drinking water for the people of Hyderabad city. SINCE THEN THERE IS NO FLOOD IN THE CITY OF HYDERABAD AND SECUNDERABAD. The people of the twin cities and the nation are indebted to Sri M. Visvesvaraya for this great plan and work.

The modern era of the development of the twin cities began soon after the last flood of the Musi river in AD 1908 which had shattered the life of the people living in Hyderabad. This necessitated planned development of the city in a phased manner. Who was the expert appointed post disaster? Sri M. Visvesvaraya of Mysore. The great engineer statesman as the book on hand counts. He submitted his report on October 1st 1909 with recommendations on preventing and recurrence of floods also improving civic amenities.

A spout of planned growth happened under Nizam VII . A city improvement trust was constituted in 1912. The wide Pathergatti bazar from the south bank of Musi to Charminar with shops on the ground and flats on the first floor was the first to be laid. It remains as one of the widest bazars in the country today ' writes Luther.

Next was the construction of Osman sagar Reservoir and Himayat sagar. Their lakes not only prevented the flooding of the river Musi but also served as reservoirs for drinking water for the city.

The state High court was built in red and white stone in Saracenic style and is a fine specimen of architecture. The designer was Shankarlal, a Rajasthani architect. Opposite to the court was built Osmania Hospital. Do you know that Osmania University was the first with an Indian language as the medium of instruction? Hyderabad was the first state in India to set up a Public sector unit – The Road Transport Department.

BRIEF HISTORY OF HYDERABAD

Visvesvaraya submitted another report in 1930 consisting of 25 pages. It presaged the Master Plan of Hyderabad promulgated finally in 1977 as Luther informs "It suggests the modern city concepts of outer and inner ring roads, zoning, Slum clearance, sewerage and drainage schemes construction of markets at a cost of 44.7 million.

In 1930 the state museum came up in a palace constructed in 1864. In the public garden . It seems the Nizam has built it for one of his daughter, which was called 'the doll's house'. However due to superstition she did not occupy the palace. A specialty of the museum as Luther writes in that it is the only museum in the country with the similarities of the Ajanta paintings "The manuscript section includes a copy of Quran bearing the seal of Emperor Shah Jahan.

Wikipedia page on Hyderabad narrates that Musi River's claim to fame is its significance in the birth of the city of Hyderabad. The fifth ruler of Golconda Muhammad Quli Qutubshah fell in love with a local dancer named Baghmati. She lived in a village of Chichlam situated in the southern bank of Musi.

When yet a prince he used to meet her braving the floods of Musi. Later they were married and the prince ascended the throne. "When the fort of Golconda becomes insufficient and there was shortage of water and other resources the emperor decided to shift his capital to the village of Chichlam and thus Hyderabad was born in year 1591.

CHIEF ENGINEER OF MYSORE

Soon after his first retirement from Government of British post at Aden he was appointed as Chief Engineer of Mysore state in November 1909. He took up the job of Chief Engineer as he was very eager to serve his home state and was very interested in tackling challenging cases.

Sir M.Visvesvaraya is recognized for engineering the Krishna Raja Sagar dam located near Mysore. He was also secretary to the Railways and was instrumental in laying the new railway lines across the then Mysore state.

He has earned a reputation for his honesty, integrity, ability and intelligence.

THE KING, THE DAM AND THE GARDENS

THE KING

Nalwadi Krishnaraja Wodiyar was the twenty fourth maharaja of the Kingdom of Mysore from1894 to till his death in 1940. The King wanted to help the farmers of Mysore and Mandya as they had repeated crop failures because of dry region and famine. The King discussed his desire to help the farmers at any cost. The then Chief Engineer of Mysore Sri M Visvesvaraya presented a blue print of dam which would be constructed across Kaveri River near Karnambadi village. But the cost construction of the dam was very high and the finance department of the Government of Mysore rejected the proposal.

The King became depressed and sad. His wife Maharani Pratap Kumari Ammani donated all her jewelry to the King and asked him to fulfill all his desires. On hearing about the queen donating all her jewelry all the people of Mysore including the rich and the poor started donating money and jewelry for the noble cause of dam construction. All the corpus money was with the King and he asked Sir M Visveswaraya to start the dam construction.

Mysore was under Madras residency which rejected the King's proposal of the construction of the dam but Sir M Visveswaraya persistently pursued the British Government and got its approval.

The construction of the KRS dam in 1911 and ended in1932.

KRS DAM AND SIR MV

- Krishna Raja Sagara Dam is also known as KRS Dam near Mysore. Krishna Raja Sagar is a town in Mandya district in the Indian state of Karnataka. Named after Krishna Raja sagar Wodeyar lV. KRS Dam was built by Chief engineer of Mysore Sri M.Visveshwaraya under his rule. KRS dam was built in 1924 across Cauvery riverbnear the joining of three rivers viz; Cauvery, Hemavathi, and Laxmana Theerdha.

- KRS dam is a gravity dam of stone masonry with a height of 130.80ft . It has gross storage of capacity of 49.45TMC. It was a project initially designed to supply water for drinking and irrigation for Mysore and Mandya. Later, now it has become the major source of water for the City of Bangalore, which has grown faster.

- KRS town was earlier known as Kannambadi, hence KRS dam is also locally called as the Kannambadi Katte. As per legends this place is said be the same place were sage Kanva lived hence this Kannambadi was also called as Kanvapuri.

- KRS dam water further flows to Mettur dam in Tamilnadu. River Cauvery joins Bay of Bengal in Pompuhar. There is a controversy between two states viz; Karnataka and Tamilnadu regarding sharing of river Cauvery water, and

Supreme Court has formed a special Cauvery Tribunal which decides the amount of water to be shared by both the states. The 48 Automatic gates of the KRS dam are at 114 feet level. New crest gates are installed at plus 80 feet level. Dr Gundappa in his book 'Mysoorina Diwanaru' stated that it was because of Sir MV, the height of the dam was raised to 124 feet, from its original idea of 80 feet. It was a bold decision taken by Sir MV and also got the approval from British Government.

BRINDAVAN GARDENS

Brindavan gardens which is adjacent to KRS dam is one of the major tourist places near Mysore. Brindavan gardens are famous for the world famous water dance. KRS dam is at a distance of 20Km from Mysore. This dam has become the life line for many people on the banks of the Cauvery River. One should visit the Brindavan gardens in the evening hours to enjoy the colorful water dance.

There is a guest house a state run hotel and luxury hotel for the tourist who visits the famous spot every day and the people are indebted to Sir MV for this immortal project.

DIWAN OF MYSORE

After Tippu Sultan, the concept of Diwans was conceived in the Kingdom of Mysore with Diwan Purnaiah as the first ever Prime Minister of the Kingdom of Mysore, who was a Diwan for Tipu sultan. And after the end of the sultans he reported to the Maharaja of Mysore his highness Krishna Raja Wadiyar III.

The word Diwan in Urdu means the Prime Minister of the Kingdom, more precisely a royal advisor to the monarch Sir M. Visveshwaraiah was appointed as Diwan of Mysore from Nov 1912 –Dec 1918 under the King Nalwadi Krishna Raja Wadiyar. Sir M.V was preceded by T.Anand Rao and succeeded by M.KanthaRaj Urs.

When Sir M Visvesvaraya was offered the position of Dewan of Mysore State it is said that he invited all his relatives for a grand dinner. After the dinner he told them that he would accept the offer on only one condition that his relatives should not come to him for any help nor to get their personal work done.

During his service as Dewan of Mysore he founded eminent institutions like

Mysore Soap factory,

Bangalore Agricultural University

State Bank of Mysore

Mysore Iron and Steel Works

Mysore bulb factory etc. etc.

During his tenure itself the Outlook of Mysore changed because of various small and medium scale industries.

He founded the first Engineering College- Government Engineering College in Bangalore in 1917. Now it is known as Visvesvaraya College of Engineering. He had introduced compulsory education in the state which latter was embroided as the fundamental right in the Constitution of Independent India.

During this stint as the diwan of Mysore he revamped the state into what was then came to be known as a model state. He was also called the Father of modern Mysore.

Other notable contributions of Sir M. Visveshwaraya include

Hindustan Aeronauticals Limited

Mysore Lamps

Mysore chemicals and fertilizers ltd

Mysore Paper Mills

Mysore Paints and Varnish Ltd

Hydro Electric Power Plants on Sivana Samudra Falls and Jog falls

Bangalore was the first city in India to get Streetlights in 1905.

UNIVERSITY OF MYSORE

The University of Mysore is a public state University in Mysore, Karnataka. The University was founded during the reign of Nalwadi Krishna Raja Wodeyar IV; the Maharaja of Mysore. It opened on 27th July 1916. The first Chancellor was the Maharaja of Mysore; the first Vice Chancellor was H.V.Nanjundaiah. It was opened during the tenure of Sir M.V as the Dewan of Mysore. He felt that only education can change the destiny of a human being or a country. Sir M.V's favorite statement that 'Nothing is equal to knowledge' stands as a motto in English of the University of Mysore.

STATE BANK OF MYSORE

State Bank of Mysore was a Public sector Bank in India with headquarters at Bengaluru. It was one of the five associate banks of SBI.

State Bank of Mysore was established in the year 1913 as The Bank of Mysore and was founded on 2nd October 1913 by Sir M. Visveswaraya. It has 2074 branches and 9 extensions. The bank was affectionately called Mysore Bank or Namma Bank. Now after 104 years of banking history State Bank of Mysore walks into sunset after merger with State Bank of India in the year 2017 on April 1st.

BHADRAVATHI IRON AND STEEL WORKS

Bhadravathi is an industrial city and taluk in Shivamoga district of Karnataka State India. It is situated at a distance of 255Km from Bangalore and 20 Km from Shivamogga.

Town of Bhadravathi is famous for steel plant called Visvesvaraya Iron and Steel Limited, which was earlier known as Mysore Iron Steel Limited.

Bhadravathi derives its name from the Bhadra River which flows through the city. This in English means city of fire (Venkipura).In Karnataka it is also called Benki Pattana.

During his tenure as Diwan of Mysore Sri M Visvesvaraya made an attempt to start the Industrial development by preparing plan to setup Mysore Iron and Steel works at Bhadravathi. He took help of Mr. C.P.Perrin an American Consulting Engineer and expert who had designed the Tata Iron and steel works at Jamshedpur. He approved the scheme and construction started in 1918. He suggested that Hydroelectricity would be generated from Gersoppa falls and conveyed to Iron works. Construction works done by Perrin and Marshal of New York who had to get the machinery also.

Sri M Visvesvaraya had already prepared the blue print of the company and when things were going in order he decided to retire from Mysore service as differences started arising between the Maharaja Krishnaraja Wodiyar and himself.

The Mysore Gazette issued on this occasion stated that during this period Sri M Visvesvaraya labored with single minded devotion to increase the material resources of the state. His administration as Dewan of Mysore has resulted in educational, irrigational technological industrial and Railways incredible progress and he had laid the foundations for a prosperous and progressive future for the State.

Mysore Iron and steel works had a unique distinction of being the biggest state owned company in south India. It was the first in India to establish fero silicone plant and electric pig iron for furnaces. Bhadravathi came to be called as the Birmingham of South India.

PARTICIPATION IN POLITICAL AND OTHER CONFERENCES

A committee of Dewan's and Princes was constituted in 1917. Sri M. Visvesvaraya as a Dewan of entire State he conducted important meetings with members from all Indian states and took their suggestions.

He attended Indian Science congress at Lucknow in 1923.

He also attended Indian economic conference and gave his suggestions.

Members of newly elected court of Indian Institute of Science Bangalore elected Visvesvaraya as its president from 1938 for a total period of 9 successive years. It is considered as one of the longest tenures as President in the history of Indian Institute of Science.

In 1922 he participated in the all parties meet where he interacted actively. He gave his ideas to the then President of Indian National Congress, Chitaranjan Das, he also spoke to Pandit Madan Mohan Malaviya, M A Jinna, M R Jayakar, Mahatma Gandhi and Ms. Annie Besant. When Prince of Wales visited India, he was the main Chairman of the Conference. He acted like a bridge between the Indian National Congress and the British Government.

He was also the Chairman of the South Indian States People's conference held in Trivandrum in the year 1929.

Sir M V worked day and night to attend as many conferences as possible. He gave his suggestions in the conferences to the committee members of the entire country, and saw to that they were implemented as soon as possible with his persistent follow up.

FOREIGN TOURS

Visveswaraya was fond of foreign tours not because of holidaying or recreation. His main aim was to gather information from the advanced or developed countries and use them skillfully in our country again by cost cutting without compromising on the quality.

In 1898 itself, in his initial posting at Bombay he visited Japan for 3 months. He was impressed by the people of Japan who worked hard for increasing the production and economy of the country and takes the country forward.

In 1908 he again visited Europe and America. His main interest was to study engineering innovations on water supply, dam construction, prevent soil erosion, drainage solutions. And latest engineering works. His visits included the following countries for up gradation of his knowledge…..

Canada

Denmark

London

Holland

Colombo

Singapore

Hong Kong

Shanghai

Nagasaki

Detroit

Birmingham

Washington

Italy

Germany

Sweden

He used to maintain a dairy with all the up to date information during his tour. After his return he read his book again and implemented them in India.

He advised the young engineers to go to foreign countries not to settle there but to earn knowledge and come back to India and use them for common good of our people.

In 1920 he was appointed as a member of Bombay reclamation committee and posted at London to study about steel manufacturing. He was successful in selling charcoal dig iron from Bhadravathi to the American business delegates who had attended at London business meet. A few years later he went himself studied the designs and working of automobile industry for six months at Birmingham, Italy Germany and France. He visited both the Ford and Fiat company managers with the help of whom he set up an automobile industry in Bombay.

In 1946 as a Chairman of the Indian Manufacturing organization he visited London again and made a detailed study of Textile and Chemical industries.

He visited the famous Niagara Falls Hydro static electric power stations.

Air craft factories in Bristol and Derby in 1946.

After touring the foreign countries he used the same principles with Indianization to suit our projects.

SIR MV – A MAN OF SIMPLICITY

Simplicity is the ultimate sophistication say Lenardo da vinci, around greater than four hundred years ago and Visvesvaraya was a perfect role model for simplicity and good manners.

Being a vegetarian and non-alcoholic his food habits were very simple. His lunch and dinner included small chapathis , a little rice, curd and plantain. He would not eat anything in between.

His daily routine would start around 6 am and he went for a regular cross country walks and would say to people that walking is the best exercise to get rid of all the ills. Even during his old age his servant used to run behind him with an umbrella where as he used to walk comfortably.

He loved nature and was mesmerized by the inexhaustible resources that nature provided and often felt sad when people wasted the natural resources.

He used to dress neatly from his childhood days. His motto was to be well dressed is to be well disciplined. He advised all the people working around him to be neat and clean. Cleanliness is next to Godliness he used to say repeatedly. His cooks and servants were advised to take bath daily and wear clean clothes while at work. He never tolerated untidiness even in day-to-day affairs.

Whenever he used to come across any witty sayings in the newspapers he would cut and collect them. Later he compiled and published "wise and witty sayings for children" in the year 1957at a ripe age of97.Even a single quote or proverb would change one's life he used to stress repeatedly.

Though a hard task master he always treated his officers with honesty. He would ask them to be seated , but he would meet people only in prescribed hours and after having an appointment only. Change of work is rest he said. He was democratic in approach took opinions from all concerned and then would come to a decision which was irrevocable by any chance.

He was a shy and reserved personality. He never seeked fame and popularity. He did not use Government vehicles or machinery for his personal work. He was a great lover of sports and even started sports club to encourage youngsters to take up sports.

AWARDS AND HONOURS

Sri M. Visvesvaraya was appointed companion of the order of CIE in 1911.

In 1915, Sri M. Visvesvaraya was knighted as Knight Commander of the order of the Indian Empire KCIE by British.

Bharat Ratna was conferred in the year 1955.

Honorary membership of London Institute of Engineers.

Awarded Fellowship of Indian Institute of Science Bangalore.

He was the most popular man from Karnataka, in 20th century according to a News Paper survey conducted by Prajavani.

On September 15th in 2018 Google celebrated 157th birth day anniversary of Sri M. Visvesvaraya with a Google Doodle.

Sir M. Visvesvaraya

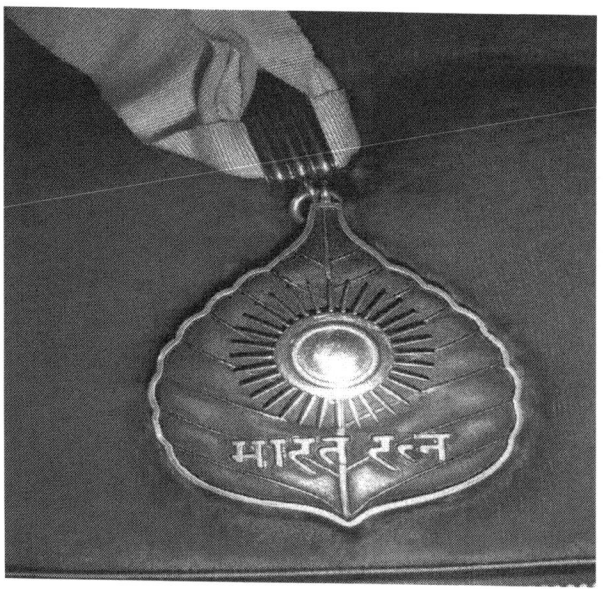

SIR M VISVESVARAYA & GANDHI

Sir M Visvesvaraya often declared Industrialize or perish but during sametime Gandhiji used to say Industrialize and perish. Even though the two great men did not have the same views about Industrialization they respected each other. In 1921 Gandhiji launched noncooperation movement which Sir M V did not agree with. In fact Sir M. Visvesvaraya would instruct Gandhiji to wear clean clothes while on tour to London for second round table conference, as he himself was immaculately dressed and believed that it adds to the personality of the individual but Gandhiji ignored his advice.

REPLY TO GANDHI

Gandhiji was of the opinion that India is a land of villages for the country to prosper he said village industries must be encouraged and is the only way to move forward Visvesvaraya said that he favored both Heavy Industries and village Industries. To the extent that you propose to develop village industries. I am at once with you. He also said that he cannot take a hostile attitude towards any constructive work from any quarter. Sri M. Visvesvaraya said I am in favor of heavy Industries because heavy industries will save the money that is going out of the country in large sums every year.

Heavy Industries are required to provide the local manufacture of machinery and equipment required by our railways and for defense forces. Heavy industries are required also for supplying machinery and tools for the village industries themselves. I recommend more extended use of mechanical power because it produces results for the country much more rapidly them human power. The object is to get food and commodities required by one people for a decent standard of living as speedily as possible.

Gandhi's appreciation for Sir M V started after seeing Bhadravathi Iron works and KrishnarajaSagara dam. It is a fine tribute to the patriotism and constructive genius of Visveswaraya who has placed his talents, knowledge and his time and energy at the service of Mysore, Gandhiji said.

In 1931 Gandhiji visited Mysore and appreciated Sir MV's contribution to Mysore for which he stated if there is a Rama rajya in modern times the title should be given to Mysore. He was also impressed with the King of Mysore Nalwadi Krishnaraja Wodeyar, for his interest in developing the state and the people of Mysore. He gave the title 'Raja rishi' to the King meaning saintly King.

SIR M V AND JAWAHARLAL NEHRU

When the first Prime Minister of India Pandit Jawaharlal Nehru congratulated Sir M. Visvesvaraya and told him that his government has decided to confer on him the Nation's highest honor viz., Bharat Ratna for his work to which Sir M. Visvesvaraya said if you feel that by giving the title I will praise your government. You will be a disappointed man because I am a fact finding man, however Pandit Jawaharlal Nehru the then Prime Minister said that he was the most deserving man and he should accept it. As Sir M. Visvesvaraya was not interested in taking any awards he reluctantly agreed upon Nehru's request. He was conferred Bharat Ratna in 1955.

Even in his nineties he was called by then Prime Minister Jawaharlal Nehru, to examine several proposals for bridges to be built over the Ganga River. Before taking up any project he used to do an aerial survey of the region. He noted the problems along with their solutions in his diary. Based on the location selected by him, a road cum Railway Bridge was built near Mokama Bihar.

Sir M. Visvesvaraya

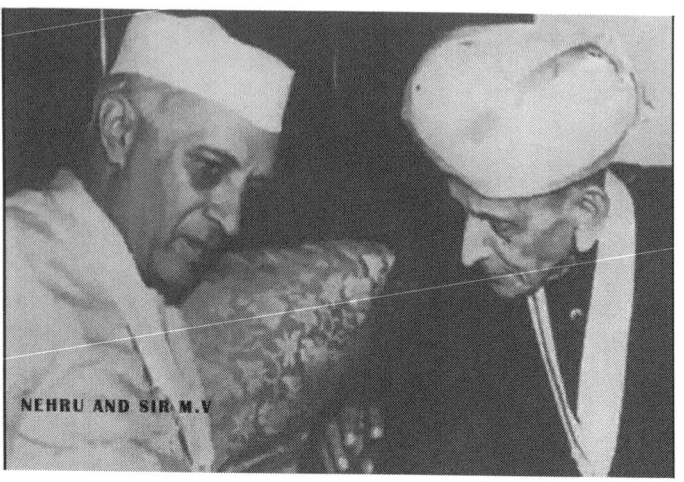

NEHRU AND SIR M.V

HUMOROUS CENTURION

When asked on his 100th birthday celebration on how he escaped the sight of Chitragupta (follower of Yama) and Yama (God of death) he used to smile and say that have you noticed on my front door that I have written "Naale Baa" meaning come home tomorrow so when Chitragupta is visiting his house he reads the statement on his door and returns back and this is how I have crossed 100 years he used to say jokingly. After hearing Visvesvaraya many local people started to write 'Naale baa' meaning come tomorrow, on their front door.

Even at that ripe age he was neatly dressed and highly punctual. He was a teetotaler from the beginning and when somebody offered him cigarettes or hot drinks he used to refuse politely and say that he is a very simple man and not so highly civilized to use them.

CENTURIAN SIR M.VISHVESVARAIAH

DEATH AND LEGACY

The great Indian Engineer Sri M Visvesvaraya died peacefully in his sleep and died a natural death on April 14th 1962 at a ripe old age of 102 he had left a powerful legacy.

He rightly said that his buildings will live after him. The famous KRS dam is a famous tourist spot of Mysore where lakhs of visitors from India and abroad visit and re live the memories of this great builder Engineer.

His Alma matter the college of Engineering Pune erected a statue in his honor.

The Visvesvaraya Industrial and Technological museum at Bangalore is named in his honor.

MUDDENA HALLI MEMORIAL

Visvesvaraya National memorial Trust manages a Memorial of Visvesvaraya at his birth place Muddenahalli. The memorial exhibits all his achievements, titles awards and personal belongings including his living room. The memorial is adjacent to his house where Sir M Visvesvaraya was born on 15th September 1860. The house is refurbished and regarded as a temple by locals.

Sir M.VISVESWARAYA'S LEGACY

Visveswaraya Institute of Technology, Coimbatore

Visveswaraya college of Engineering, Kottayam.

VisveswarayaTechnological University which is based in Belagavil, to which most of the Engineering colleges in Karnataka are affiliated.

Sri M Visveswaraya Institute of Technology, Bangalore.

Visveswaraya Institute of Engineering and Technology (VIET) Ghaziabad.

Visveswaraya Institute of Technology, Gouthambudha Nagar, UP.

Visveswaraya group of Institutions, (VGI), Greater Noida.

Visveswaraya college of Engineering and Technology, (VCET), Rangareddy.

Visveswaraya Institute of Engineering and Technology (VIET), Ghaziabad.

Visveswaraya National Institute of Technology, Nagpur.

Visveswaraya Polytechnic College, Karimnagar.

Two Metro Stations in India have been named after him;

One in Bangalore, on Purple line (Sir MV Station, Central College).

And another one in Delhi on Pink line Sir Visveswaraya Moti Bagh.

Visveswaraya Bhavan

The Institute of Engineers

Telangana State Centre

Khairathabad, Hyderabad

Various Engineering Colleges throughout the Country are named after this great engineer

TALES OF VISVESVARAYA

There are many stories about Sir M. Visvesvaraya doing the rounds in and around his birth place; some popular stories are as follows

THE TRAIN STORY

It was sometime around midnight on a fine day a train was moving towards its destination at night. A man was sleeping with his head on the side of the window in the train. Suddenly he woke up and pulled the chain over his head. The train moved for a short distance and stopped suddenly. The railway people and the passengers inside the train rushed to the compartment to know what had happened. Some people said that somebody in a sleepy mood must have pulled the chain.

But the man who pulled the chain appeared alert and told the people around him that there is a crack in the railway line few meters ahead of the train. He asked them to use torch and confirm the crack in the railway line. People surrounding him thought he was joking and did not believe the thin man.

However the railway personnel got down the apartment and observed the railway track. To their surprise they found a big crack in the railway line and thus an accident was averted.

The man who alerted the railway department was none other than Sri M Visvesvaraya.

THE CHAIR STORY

When Sir MV was Dewan of Mysore he noticed that during the world famous Mysore Dasara celebration, Britishers were sitting on the chairs and Indian officers were sitting on the floor. This type of step motherly treatment by the organizers upset Sir MV, and he told the organizers to arrange chairs for Indian officers also. He respected all people who worked for the Government immaterial of their post. He said that Government job is God's job and one must do the assigned job with utmost sincerity. During his tenure as Dewan of Mysore he arranged chairs for all the Indian officers and also provided decent sitting arrangements for the general public.

THE CAR STORY

Once Sir MV wanted to visit his native place Muddenahalli, the then Chief Minister of Karnataka, Sri Kengal Hanumanthaiah, (the Chief Architect of the world famous Bangalore Vidhan Soudha building) offered him a lift using a Government Car. But Sir MV politely refused and said that he was not on Government work to use a Government vehicle. The Chief Minister drove him in his personal car to fulfil Sir MV's desire and also proving that a friend in need is a friend in deed.

THE BRAIN STORY

It was said that brainy and intelligent students were said to have the brain of Sri M Visvesvaraya.

After Sri M Visvesvaraya's death many countries demanded the brain of our Sri M Visvesvaraya for research purposes. But our Government officials refused to accept the deal saying son of Indian soil is not for sale. They say people like Sri M Visvesvaraya used around 15-20% of the brains whereas ordinary people use only 6-8% of their brains.

These are some of the tales doing the rounds in and around Chikkaballapur town where Sri M Visvesvaraya lived his last days.

BOOKS OF SIR MV

1. Reconstructing India (1920) was published by P.S King and son
2. Planned economy for India (1936) was published by Bangalore press
3. Memories of my working life (1951) was published by Bangalore press
4. Unemployment in India ; it's causes and cure (1932) was published by Bangalore press
5. Speeches of Sir M Visvesvaraya (1917) was published by Bangalore Govt. press
6. Wise and Witty sayings for children (1957)
7. A brief memory of my complete working life (1959) was published by Bangalore Govt press

Famous quotes of Sir M Visvesvaraya

- Hard work performed in a disciplined manner wills in most cases keep the worker fit and also prolong his life.
- My buildings will be my legacy they will speak for me long after I am gone.
- Work hard, work harder, work with efficiency; work in co-operative spirit work with a team spirit to make your country great, self-supporting and strong.
- Every man who has become great owes his achievement to incessant toil.
- The way to build a nation is to build a good citizen. The majority of the citizens should be efficient, have good character and possess a reasonable high sense of duty.
- Work performed with higher knowledge or skill capacity or ambition usually brings a correspondingly higher reward.
- Self-examination not moral or spirit...But secular-that is a survey and analysis of local conditions in India and a comparative study of the same with those in other parts of the globe.
- One common slogan of the west the importance of which the Indian citizen has not

yet sufficiently grasped is "if you do not work, neither shall you eat" it is by his work that an individual is enabled to earn a living.

- Remember your work may be only to sweep a railway line but it is your duty to keep it so clean that no other crossing in the world is as clean as yours.
- I walked my way to good health.
- Engineer is a person who applies the skills and knowledge of basic science for the good of society.
- To give real service you must add something which cannot be bought or measured with money
- If you buy what you do not need you will need what you cannot buy.
- Mental energy is wasted in caste disputes and village factions
- It is better to work out than rust out.
- Work,work hard,hard work does not kill. It is the worry that kills.

Lesser known facts about Sir M. Visvesvaraya

Sir M. Visvesvaraya was born on 15th September 1861 to Telugu family settled in Muddenahalli in the princely state of Mysore.

Sir M. Visvesvaraya birthday is celebrated as Engineer's day in India.

Having lost his father in young age of fifteen he had to work hard to continue his academics.

People say Sir M Visvesvaraya would walk over 50 KM every day to attend the school and would sometimes sit under the street lamps to study at night.

He was appointed as Chief Engineer of Mysore State in 1909.

Sir M. Visvesvaraya was also nominated as the 19th Diwan of Mysore who served between 1912 to 1919.

Sir M Visvesvaraya won the people's hearts when he designed a flood prevention system for Hyderabad post the Musi River devastating floods in 1908.

He also designed a system to prevent the sea erosion at Vishakhapatnam port.

He married thrice in his life time but unfortunately each time it was a failure.

He was called the father of modern Mysore state.

Sir MV is also known as father of Indian Economic planning. In 1934 Sir M V Published a book called Planned Economy In India.

Sir M V was instrumental in charting out a plan for road construction between Tirumala and Tirupathi.

Sir M.V founded Deccan club in Pune, century club and public Library in Bangalore.

Sir MV studied, planned and designed the entire area of Jaya nagar in south Bangalore. It was the biggest and best planned layout township in Asia during those days.

He started the Bangalore press and respected journalist's freedom. He setup the Kannada Parisath for the upliftment of Kannada language.

Sir M. Visvesvaraya received 'Bharat Ratna' India's highest civilian award in 1955.

He was awarded several honorary doctorate degrees including 8 from various India's Universities.

Calcutta (1921) Patna (1944)

Allahabad (1947) Jodhpur (1958)

L.L.D conferred on him by the University of Bombay 1941, Mysore 1998, Banaras 1937 and Andhra 1953.

ENGINEERS DAY

Visvesvaraya can be compared only with himself,
for there is no other like him.
He is a very rare combination of ancient
Hindu Bhisma and modern American Ford

			H.RANGACHAR & P.KODANDA RAO

Engineer's day is observed in several countries on different dates of the year. World federation of engineering organizations have designated March 4th as "World Engineers day for a sustainable world. Previous they had also observed March 2nd as Engineers day on which few associations of engineers established in Zagreb in the year 1878 in Croatia celebrated.

Every year India celebrates the Engineers day on September 15th the birth anniversary of Sri M. Visveshvaraya.

Sri M. Visveshvaraya was India's prolific civil engineer, dam builder, economist and statesman. He was one of the most prominent builders of the 20th century. When Sri M. Visveshvaraya was the Diwan of Mysore from 1912 to 1918 he transformed the state into a 'model state'. For his numerous economic and social projects he was also called as the 'Father of the Modern Mysore'.

India is celebrating Engineers day on 15th September as a mark of remembrance and tribute to the greatest Indian engineer Bharat Ratna Mokshagundam Visveshwariah. On this day we congratulate our hard working engineers and appreciate their dexterity as well as dedication. Coincidentally the international day of democracy is also celebrated on September 15th every year.

An international woman in engineering day is celebrated on June 23rd where impressive and inspiring women in engineering career are recognized and rewarded.

India is one of the major engineering hubs across the world. Millions of Engineers are produced by the nation every year and engineering is the most sought after professional education of the modern day in our country.

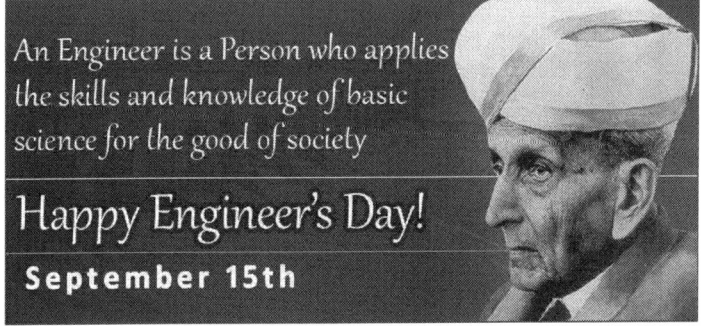

CHRONOLOGY

September 15-1860 – birth of Sir MV.

1875 Went to Bangalore to pursue BA.

1883- Graduated with civil engineering degree from Pune.

1884-PWD Engineering Bombay Residency.

1904- Honorable Membership of London Institute of Civil Engineering for an unbroken period of 50 years.

1906-Kaiser i Hind in recognition of his services.

1909-Appointed as chief Engineering of Mysore.

1911-CIE (Companion of the Indian Empire).

1912- Appointed as Dewan of Mysore.

1915- KCIE (Knight Commander of the Indian Empire).

1921- D.Sc., Calcutta University.

1931-LLD, Bombay University.

1937- D.Litt, BHU.

1943- Elected as the honorary life member of institute of Engineers India.

1944- D Sc, Allahabad University.

1948- Doctorate LLD, Mysore University.

1953- D.Litt., Andhra University.

1953- Awarded honorary fellowship by institute of Town Planners of India

1955- Awarded Bharat Ratna.

1958-D.Sc, Jodhpur University.

1958-Durga Prasad khaitan Memorial Gold Medal by the Royal Asiatic Society council of Bengal.

1959-Fellowship of Indian Institute of Science, Bangalore.

April 14 1962 – Sir M.V Passed away.

SOURCES

- Mokshagundam Visvesvaraya Engineer, statesman and planner A.V Shankar rao
- Memories of my working life 1951 published by Bangalore press.
- Visvesvaraya an engineer of modernity. The Hindu 15th September 2010.
- Our Leaders Children's Book Trust 1989 ISBN 978-81-7011-701-8
- Reconstructing India (1920) quoted in "The most celebrated Indian Engineer". Mokshagundam Visvesvaraya official website of GOI Vignan Prasar.
- Remembering the deluge of 1908. The Hindu Ifthekar J.S. 28th September, 2012.
- The Indian Express.
- Bangalore mirror
- The Avenue

SIR M.VISVESVARAYA AN INCREDIBLE ENGINEER

What do you call Sir M.Visvesvaraya. Do you call him?

An Engineer?

A Scholar?

A Statesman?

A Politician?

Or a Diwan? No doubt

He fits into all of the above and for his contributions to the people of India he was not only 'knighted as the Knight Commander of British Indian Empire (KCIE) by King George V but also awarded the Indian's highest civilian award Bharat Ratna in 1955. No wonder that his birthday on September 15th is celebrated as Engineer's Day not only in India but also in Sri Lanka and Tanzania.

A must read for all Engineers and would be engineering students from India and abroad to know about the contributions of India's most incredible engineer Sir M.Visvesvaraya.

ABOUT THE AUTHOR

Dr.R.P.RAJ, presently working as Consultant Orthopaedician at BHEL General Hospital, Hyderabad. He has done Schooling from Railway High School Hubli, MBBS from Government Karnataka Medical College Hubli, and Post-Graduation M.S Orthopedics' from the prestigious PGIMER, Chandigarh. A topper from school level he has received many awards from various institutions. He is a sought after speaker for all occasions on varied subjects.

You can mail your queries at rajkomal322@gmail.com

Whatsapp No: 9705168050

Made in the USA
Monee, IL
12 October 2022